DIVERSITY & INCLUSION

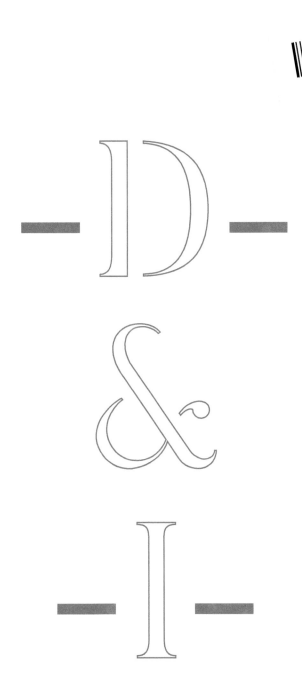

CREATED FROM OUR SOUL – UPENDO BOOKS LTD

D & I

UPENDO BOOKS LTD

Editor's Note: "Keep Rising!"

The goal for this project was to make you feel seen, heard, appreciated, respected, loved, embraced, and celebrated.

In my own educational experience, the only time that I saw someone that looked like me occurred for a few days in February. Outside of that, my culture and experience were ignored.

But this is a new day.

The young people featured will inspire and encourage you to achieve your dreams. Not the ones that you tell your friends and family, but the fragile yearnings that often are expressed only as internal whispers. I implore you to listen to them and take the steps necessary to offer your fullest selves to the world.

We desperately need your voice and leadership!

While learning about historical figures is enlightening, they are often people whose accomplishments and lives seem so far removed from ours.

This is not to say that their contributions were nominal, but only to assert that young people relate to young people. Our logic led us to a question - What is the best way to inspire our youth? And our conclusion was to focus on young people. All of them are remarkable and so are you!

–Njoroge Mungai,
UPENDO BOOKS LTD

> **" I'm not a black artist, but an artist.**

Basquiat

(1960 - 1988)

UPENDO BOOKS LTD

D & I

CONTENT

D & I

CONTENT

◇

OUR Experiences

We want you to feel seen, heard, appreciated, accepted, and EMBRACED. Your lives are important. Your dreams are important. And your VOICES are important.

Now to the content. We discussed the youths that we wanted to feature in our first edition at length. All of us are proud to say that everyone featured is REMARKABLE.

Yes, they have gifts. Yes, some of them are genetically predisposed to excel. But NONE of them coasted. Each person honed their gifts and then used them to uplift others.

That is our challenge to you.

Be great. Dream big. Then dream Bigger. Then accomplish those goals. You are GREAT!

Work on your *DREAMS* Now

CREW LOVE

We are so fortunate to work with so many talented, diligent, creative, loving, kind, appreciative, funny and incredibly intelligent people.

Thank you all for your energy, love, and dedication. It brought this project to life.

We ADORE each one of you!!!

FOUNDER/PUBLISHER
NJOROGE M

My message to every reader is simple. Work on your dream every day. Take small steps but make sure they are consistent.

In a few months you will be shocked at the progress that you have made through the sheer power of momentum.

Stay focussed. And if you are so inclined, get in touch.

We would love to feature you in our next edition.

EDITOR IN CHIEF
CHRISTINA M

My message to the reader is one that could be hard to swallow.

Surround yourself with ONLY well wishers.

Stay away from those that deride your goals.

Constructive criticism is useful but not if the comments are personal in nature.

Sometimes even family members need to be loved at a distance.

It's OK. Every successful person at some point has had to sequester themselves.

It is a difficult path to follow emotionally, but one that will serve you well in the long run.

Love others.

Give without expectation of receiving.

Live in GREATNESS!

We know you will do amazing things with your life.

BUSINESS
MAYA A

My message to the reader is hopeful.

Nothing is impossible.

Everything that surrounds you was developed by someone that used their talents to bring their vision to life.

The only thing that separates those that achieve their «DREAMS» from those that don't isn't intelligence, skill, time, resources, ect. It is an unwavering belief that they will achieve their goals coupled with a set of consistent behaviours.

You deserve a life that you LOVE and there is only one path to achieve it - HARD WORK.

Get lost in the beauty of incremental progress. It's not sexy. It's not something that you see on social platforms, but nothing worthwhile is achieved in an instant.

Revel in the person you're becoming in perusing your dreams.

SALES DIRECTOR
ROBERT S

My message to the reader is pragmatic.

Learn to sell.

Period.

You could be the most esoteric artist, but if you want to be successful, you will not be able to avoid learning the process of extending an offer and then iterating your approach based on the prospect's reaction.

Develop a compelling pitch for your book, painting, skill set, ect.

Think about the problem that you want to solve.

Get very SPECIFIC.

Develop an avatar of your PERFECT client.

And then uncover the places that they frequent (online and in real life).

Talk to them about their struggles and help them overcome each one.

Remember, wealth isn't created by taking value, but by giving it.

GRAPHIC DESIGNER
AARON D

My message to the reader is appreciative.

Love art!

Revel in creativity.

Take a few moments each day to dissect the things that make your heart sing and spirit feel light.

Even if you aren't inclined to love brush strokes, movement, vocal undulations, or dramatic situations, my advice is to observe LIFE.

Look at the people around you and develop backstories about their existence and emotional reactions.

The point is to be an active participant in the rich tapestry that is woven around us at every moment.

We call it being ALIVE.

My challenge to you is to smile at a stranger that isn't creepy. After they smile back, let us know if you still prefer to scroll through your device.

OUR VOICES RESONATE

SPIKE LEE
FILMMAKER

He proved to me that being an artist while uplifting others wasn't impossible.

Seeing Malcolm X changed my life.

It was a gorgeous piece of art that inspired my appreciation not only for the technical aspects of writing a flawless script but also for the sense of responsibility one incurred by being a storyteller.
I love Spike for being such a genius and demanding that all artists dedicate themselves to improving their craft.

TONY KUSHNER
PLAYWRIGHT

Imaginative. Brave. Intelligent. Emotionally touching. These words best describe his work.

Tony taught me the power of humanizing my creations.

Angels in America was a revelation. 7 hours! I never thought that any piece of art would hold my attention for that long. And not only was I on the edge of my seat for the duration, but after it ended, I wanted more.

He is a true master at helping us empathise with everyone.

CHARLIE KAUFMAN
FILMMAKER

Eternal Sunshine of the Spotless Mind changed my life. A story about erasing the memory of a romantic relationship was revelatory.

I laughed. I cried. And then I told everyone about this «quirky» film. But the one thing that I was not able to get over was a simple question.

Would I erase anyone from my memory? And then the answer arrived. I already had. And I wasn't alone.

This forced me to get off of auto-pilot during interactions.

STAY INSPIRED

Through their work, these ARTISTS and many others helped us CREATE this offering. We want you to realise your DREAMS and UPLIFT others.

TRACY K. SMITH
POET

Her words. God. Her words!

The feeling that lingered after reading her masterful work, Life on Mars was gratitude.

Humanity and our existential angst are captured with such honesty that it will cause you to question the meaning of «progress» and its applicability to our species.

As you read every piece, reflect on your thoughts and experiences. This practice will alter your reality in the most profound and glorious ways!

LINA IRIS VIKTOR
VISUAL ARTIST

She is the type of artist whose bold visions inspire the viewer to push their creative boundaries.

Seeing a black woman rendered with such respect and adulation was the medicine that I needed during a difficult period in my life.

She inspired me to continue painting at a time when I had given up all hope of being creative again.

Do yourself a favour and view her work today.

MISTY COPELAND
BALLERINA

Her documentary, A Ballerina's Tale is mandatory viewing in my book.

Watching Misty address being estranged from her mother was heartbreaking. If this wasn't brutal enough, she also was battling a physical injury that threatened to end her career while being under the unforgiving eye of the media.

Despite all of this, she made history. Misty became the first African American female principal dancer with the American Ballet Theatre.

CREATE NOW

The

D&I
PODCAST

ANN
Y. K CHOI

CHACHO
VALADEZ

CHRISTON
"THE TRUTH" JONES

WE INTERVIEW THE
MOST TALENTED AND
FASCINATING GUESTS

Our Voices

https://anchor.fm/upendobooks

UPENDO BOOKS LTD

Our Healing

Dasia Taylor, an 18 year old from Iowa developed a holistic way of treating infections that will save millions of lives worldwide

O ur ailments can be healed with the remedies that exist within nature. Dasia Taylor, an 18 year old from Iowa not only concurs but also has developed a novel approach to addressing medical infections, a serious yet preventable malady that affects hundreds of millions of people around the world.

According to data from the Agency for Healthcare Research and Quality (AHRQ), more than 10 million people undergo surgical procedures as inpatients in the United States. This accounts for one fourth of all hospital stays. Unfortunately, these people might suffer from surgical site infections.

WHERE DOES THIS TYPE OF COMPLICATION OCCUR?

This type of complication occurs close to the incision site within 30 days or 90 if the surgery involves prosthetics.

Although these infections are preventable, approximately two to four million people experience surgical site infections. The AHRQ states that up to three million people will die due to this complication.

The key to saving these lives depends on swift identification and effective treatment. Even though this issue confounded medical professionals, Dasia was unintimidated.

HOW DID DASIA DISCOVER THE SUTRES THAT SHE NEEDED?

She found an article detailing the ability of sutures to communicate the status change of a wound through the shift of electrical resistance within the skin and everything changed. She saw a way forward. The article noted that any fluctuations in the electrical resistance were relayed to smartphones belonging to patients as well as doctors.

While this approach is promising, it provides a barrier to effective treatment for anyone without reliable internet connections.

This inequity inspired Dasia to develop a solution that was more holistic and equitable. During her research, she learned that healthy skin is naturally acidic and has a pH that is about 5. An infected wound increases that pH to 9.

"Knowing that I have inspired people all over the world is the real prize to me"

Now, pH levels can be detected without the use of electronics.

In fact, many natural sources such as vegetables as well as fruits alter their colour based on pH levels.

While experimenting, Dasia noticed that bright red beets changed their colour at the same pH level that indicated a site infection.

She reasoned that if she applied the dye from beets to the type of thread surgeons used to secure sutures, a surgical site infection could be confirmed. This was a REMARKABLE accomplishment. But now, Dasia had to find the type of thread that could hold onto the dye.

WHAT MADE SOLVING THIS PROBLEM CHALLENGING?

One - The thread that she selected needed to hold onto the dye as it changed colour based on the pH level of the patient's skin.

Two - The thread needed to have the same thickness as regular surgical thread.

After weeks of testing, she found that a cotton-polyester blend met both requirements.

Under infection-like conditions, this thread retained the colour of the beet - it changed from bright red to dark purple.

Dasia knew that this indicated an infection.

Although this was a "difficult" problem to solve, Dasia tackled it step at a time. She advises others to adopt this approach.

Interview

FAIR TRADE

Christon "The Truth" Jones is a multi-million dollar stock investor and he's ready to help you become wealthy too

Financial freedom affords us the opportunity to dedicate our time to pursuits that inspire our growth rather than inhibit it. Issues pertaining to obligation dissipate while opportunities to flourish abound. Becoming wealthy is not difficult. It only requires a certain temperament. This belief is espoused by Christon "The Truth" Jones, a multi-millionaire not yet out of his teens. Any inquisitive reader will wonder about the strategy that Christon employed to reach financial independence. He, like many others before him, leveraged the power of the stock market. More specifically, he focussed on stock options.

There are two types of options: calls and puts.

Stay Focussed

"You can't wish for a better life, you have to create it!"

Christon "The Truth" Jones

A call option is a contract that gives the option buyer the right but not the obligation to buy or sell the underlying asset by a certain date (expiration date) at a specified price (strike price).

A put option is an option to sell assets at an agreed price on or before a particular date.

HOW CAN WE REACH FINANCIAL ABUNDANCE?

It requires a shift in mindset. To him, it means investing in companies rather than only consuming the products that they manufacture.

His investment strategy is outlined by an acronym that guided him to financial independence. He notes it is possible for anyone to reach their investment goals if they follow the T.R.U.T.H.

T – "Tap 20 companies that you really like. Be sure to choose companies in which you already buy their stuff"

R – "Research these companies and find everything that you can about them. Read AND watch the news"

U – "Understand the company's historical data. How has it been performing in the past? There could be key indicators to predict its future performance"

T – "Trade AFTER closing. Investing can be an emotional roller coaster. Sleep on it and trade the next day"

H – "Have an entry & exit strategy. Know what your bottom line numbers are, to determine when you will buy the stock and when you have hit your profit number so you get out. And stick to it!"

HOW IS CHRISTON GIVING BACK?

Given Christon's immense wealth and youth, one might assume that he would only be interested in the garish accouterments of wealth. Instead, he is focused on making a positive difference in his community.

"My dream is to open a homeless shelter".

To actualize this philanthropic ambition, he created an organisation called Truth Playmakers with his younger sister, Bailey.

He describes this group as "a 501(c)(3) entity that empowers, inspires and guides gifted youth to create generational wealth by utilising their gifts".

To recognize the accomplishments of the members, Christon invites them to an exclusive gala attended by powerful influencers, respected business leaders, and political titans. Those being honoured also have the opportunity to be mentored by successful professionals in various fields.

Christon remains busy, but all of his projects invigorate him. With a wistful smile, he describes the next twenty years of his life.

"In 2024, I will have graduated from high school with a 4.0 GPA, received a full scholarship in business to attend my school of choice, the University of South Florida. Upon graduating from college, I want to teach professional athletes how to invest so that when they leave their professional sport they do not leave broke."

WHAT ARE SOME AVENUES THAT CHRISTON RECOMMENDS FOR INCREASING WEALTH WITHIN 5 YEARS?

Christon advises that you look into options trading, crypto, and real estate. He has been widely successful in the stock market but is also aware of the abundant opportunities that exist with owning property and fungible tokens.

One other thing that is important to Christon is self-education. The two books that he recommends to everyone are: Think and Grow Rich by Napolean Hill and Money Master the Game by Tony Robbins.

WHAT TYPE OF IMPACT DOES SETTING A POSITIVE INTENTION AND VISUALISATION HAVE ON HIS LIFE?

Christon notes that picturing your goals makes an immense difference. He advises everyone to see and feel their successes before they occur.

Movement

Plié to Progress

Calvin Royal III is altering the face of ballet one stage at a time

Choreography contextualises emotion through inspired movement. Each gesture signifies cohesion or chaos. It is through these renderings that catharsis is inculcated. Yet many dancers continue to struggle for recognition. Despite this fact, some mavens of movement like Calvin Royal III are fighting for their place on the plinth of perfected performance. Despite becoming the first African-American male Principal Dancer with the American Ballet Theatre in over twenty years, Calvin is not resting on his laurels.

HOW DID CALVIN'S JOURNEY IN BALLET BEGIN?

He started training at the age of 14. In other professions, Calvin would be perceived as precocious, but in the world of ballet, he was considered a late bloomer. This made his ascent that much more unlikely.

While reflecting on his journey, Calvin recounts the difficulties he encountered.

"It was challenging on so many levels, not just being the only black kid in my class but being away from home for the first time... I felt this sense of, 'Ok, I'm an adult now at 17'. That's a lot to kind of settle in with".

"

Dance for yourself.
If someone
understands, good.
If not, it doesn't
matter.
"

To excel, he focused on refining his skills. Every day he improved different aspects of his craft. This type of diligence, discipline, and meticulous attention to detail opened up opportunities for him. Eventually, he earned leading roles in prominent productions such as Von Rothbart and Serenade After Plato's Symposium.

Calvin's performances in these productions were celebrated for their elegance and impeccable grace.

Even with these successes, he remains focussed on his true mission.

"I always knew that because I didn't see people who looked like me at the top, I wanted to get there so I could help to bridge the gap and open that door".

Calvin is still perfecting his craft. Referring to an upcoming production, he draws a parallel to his development as an artist.

"The process of learning, is, in many ways a direct reflection of my life growing up in this company and finding out what it is that I want to say as an artist and becoming this man of action and a leader. Yes, that's what this whole process is like for me".

His current success belies an occurrence that nearly derailed all the progress that he had made. In his sophomore year, he injured his back in a car accident and wasn't able to participate in any classes. Yet he remained optimistic. During this difficult time he practiced "visualising dance in his mind".

This served him well. After reaching his juniour year, he competed in Youth Amercia Grand Prix. There he was spotted by some professors at the American Ballet Theatre Jacqueline Kennedy Onassis School.

After studying there for two years, he was promoted to the main company. Unfortunately, during this time, Calvin began to have doubts and wondered if his professors would ever see him as a leading man.

Fortunately, a culture shift occurred at the company and this alteration in attitude benefitted Calvin. Despite being in a more accepting

> "It's about me being the best I can be in an art form I love and inspiring other people"

environment, he stayed focussed on improving his craft. These efforts paid off. A venerated choreographer noted that while many talented dancers reprised the same role, none had moved with the "poetry of Calvin".

HOW DOES CALVIN RELATE TO HIS AUDIENCE?

While many dancers avoid interacting with the public after their performances, Calvin is open to participating in meaningful exchanges. One encounter almost left him in tears.

A young man approached Calvin and thanked him for being a role model. Calvin's voice breaks as he describes this interaction.

"I just got the chills all over my body because it's about me being the best I can be as an artist and that in turn inspires someone else."

WHAT DOES CALVIN DO TO STAY INSPIRED?

During the pandemic, he got involved with some outside projects that fed his insatiable imagination and yearning to offer something new to his audicnce. It is this type of dedication to serving his creative muses that cause others to view his performances as transcendent.

Looking back over his accomplishments, it seems almost predestined that he ascended to the position he now holds. Calvin disagrees. His advice for his peers is resolute. "Pay your dues".

Many may view his accomplishments as occurring in rapid succession, but Calvin notes that he was still an understudy four years into his tenure at the American Ballet Theatre.

Due to his frustration, he thought about leaving his company. It was then that the artistic director nominated him for a scholarship.

He won the scholarhsip and used the $50,000 to travel across Europe and train with companies including Paris Opera, the Royal Ballet in London, and the Mariinsky Theatre in St. Petersburg.

There are a few voices that speak with the vocabulary that Calvin is mastering, and it is this ability to refine his craft that sets him apart. While luck has played a role in his success, Calvin relies more on his work ethic.

We are all fortunate that he is only beginning to soar.

Interview

BRUSH *UP*

At 18 years old, Cliffannie Forrester was an unknown artist. And then everything changed.

Her transcendent piece, Uganda was featured in the Metropolitan Museum of Art.

She was inspired to create this painting after returning from a missionary trip in Uganda. While reviewing the images that she captured while abroad, she was taken by a picture of a young girl in peaceful repose.

"We were going to church and I saw a little girl who was just standing around, admiring everything".

Inspiration

UGANDA

UPENDO BOOKS LTD

While Cliffannie was working on her piece, one of her teachers suggested that she enter P.S. Art, a competition that identifies and then places transcendent works of creativity at the Metropolitan Museum of Art.

She followed the advice of her instructor and then waited for a response. Once Cliffannie received confirmation that her portrait was selected, she shared this life changing news on social media.

The attention that she received was well deserved. Her piece was one of the 90 pieces of art that were selected from a pool of more than 1,200 submissions. Cliffannie was quick to thank her teacher for the guidance that she extended. In describing her work, Cliffannie becomes wistful.

"When I was creating Uganda I struggled to re-create the color scheme and contrasts from my references. I fused the background with the foreground in cool tones so that everything I used appears seamless in the painting."

In viewing her amazing work, it's easy to imagine the inspiration that brought it to life.

For those thinking that after achieving this monumental goal Cliffannie put away her brushes, she is quick to set the record straight. She is now working even harder and with more vigilance to get more of her work in various museums.

Tyler Gordon concurs with Cliffannie's view of staying focused on achieving successive goals despite being "successful".

The art of this 17 year old savant has been featured on the cover of TIME magazine and many other publications.

His foray into the world of creative expression began with a haunting vision.

"At ten years old, I had a dream of God telling me if I didn't use my talent, he would take it away from me".

Shaken by this premonition, he ran into the room of his mother, Nicole Kindle and regaled her with the details of his dream. She consoled him but thought that it was a singular event. Unfortunately, Tyler had the same nightmare over the next couple of days.

> "My next goal is to get another piece in a museum."

Nicole purchased Tyler's first canvas, set of brushes, and tubes of paint.

Tyler's nightmares dissipated but his work ethic intensified. While he had a natural gift for painting, he never relented in pushing himself to learn more about his craft. He painted with an obsession that helped to radically improve his technique. Once he reached a level of heightened proficiency through his daily practice, he received requests for commissions for his work.

Now, Tyler is a sought after artist and his pieces are procured by world renowned creatives, athletes, and business moguls.

Tyler is humbled by all of the accolades that he has earned, but the praise of one supporter continues to inspire him, Vice President Kamala Harris.

He still remembers the humility that she demonstrated during their initial conversation.

"Even though it was right before Thanksgiving and she's the Vice President, she was still at home cooking cornbread with her family. It really inspired me to stay humble and keep pushing forward".

While many are dazzled by Tyler's artistic ability, it is his unwavering resolve to overcome a physical challenge that makes him special.

For the first six years of his life, Tyler was deaf. Although this condition has regressed, it left him with a slight stutter.

Despite his speech impediment, Tyler continues to ascend. And his hard work continues to be rewarded.

Recently, he was named a runner up in the TIME Magazine/Nickelodeon "Kid of The Year" campaign. He was also commissioned to paint Lebron James for a cover story in Time Magazine. It was an honour that Tyler still appreciates since Lebron is one of his favourite athletes.

Tyler's portrait of the Central Park Five sold for more than $100,000 at auction. He also Won a 2020 Global Child Prodigy and received a Runner up prize for the TIME Magazine/Nickelodeon – Kid of the Year Award.

Both Cliffannie and Tyler remind us that the most "gifted" artists are never content to rely on their talents alone. These creatives work diligently to hone their craft every day.

OUR STEM

Alena Wicker, a 14 year old from Arizona, has become the youngest black person in history to be accepted into the University of Alabama's Heersink School of Medicine. She will be part of the 2024 cohort.

Her journey to achieving this monumental distinction began as a high school student who loved puzzles. She showed an affinity for engineering at an early age. Her mother recalls fondly Alena's declaration at four years old that one day she would work at NASA. In discussing her accomplishments, Alena notes that she is not exceptional. "I'm a normal person". She does credit her success to other attributes.

"I just have extremely good time management skills and I'm very disciplined."

HOW DID ALENA DEVELOP HER MOTIVIATION?

Being a conscientious youth, Alena wanted to model herself after a successful African American woman in a STEM related field. During her research to find one, she was disheartened to discover not even a handful.

Rather than allowing this discovery to derail her dreams, she launched her own website, Brown Stem Girl. To date, it has over 400 members and there are now 2,000 on the waiting list. On it, Alena educates young women of colour about various aspects of STEM and provides advice on excelling in these demanding fields. This platform also offers financial scholarships, mentorship programs, and additional resources to standout students.

WHAT DOES SHE WANT TO ACCOMPLISH IN MEDICAL SCHOOL?

"A big part of what I want to do is viral immunology, and I want to advocate for underrepresented communities that lack health care. This is something that I've become passionate about."

Alena will continue to inspire others through various ventures. She has been doing speaking engagements for years and has received numerous honours and awards. In 2021, she became NASA's youngest intern and followed up this fantastic accomplishment by being a finalist for Time Magazine's Top Kid of The Year in 2022.

Alena plans on being a doctor by her 18th birthday.

"It doesn't matter how old you are. You can do it! Don't let anybody tell you no."

Another young achiever focused on inspiring her peers is Temple Lester, a 16 year old from Atlanta Georgia. To encourage more of her peers to get excited about STEM, she created STEM Swag Box.

In this kit there are various activities and experiments that are not only fun but also engaging. Creating this kit, however, was only the first step for Temple. She knew that maintaining the enthusiasm for data driven disciplines, young people like her needed continual exposure to it, so developed a personalised approach.

WHY DOES TEMPLE LOVE STEM?

Although it is difficult for Temple to identify the precise moment that she was exposed to STEM, her love for it developed out of an insatiable curiosity.

"When I was 7 or 8, I convinced my Dad to turn his 'man cave' into my science lab. The thing I love most about STEM is that it allows me to solve, investigate, and come up with solutions"

WHAT DOES TEMPLE WANT TO ACCOMPLISH?

"I created my website first in 2016 when I was nine years old to encourage my peers to take an interest in STEM by doing these cool DIY/ science videos. This idea came from my time at a science summer camp where I was the only girl and one of few minorities. The camp counselors kept calling me their little "princess". STEM Girl Swag came a few years later, to show people how cool "science lovers" and "nerds" can be. I can be smart and dope at the same time. My mission is to increase inclusion in STEM while making it fun and available to all. My STEM Swag Box is the coolest science kit ever! It is exploding with seven different hands-on experiments. I wanted to create something that could make STEM-education fun".

As far as her role model, Temple acknowledges her mother. "My mom is my first role model. She is a psychotherapist, entrepreneur, and public speaker. I've learned so much about advocating for myself and others from her. I also look up to Danni Washington, she is an ocean advocate and she's blazing a trail in the Science Communicator field"

Temple like Alena was a finalist for Time Magazine's Kid of The Year Award (2022).

UPENDO BOOKS LTD

Visible LIGHT

Tyler Mitchell made history by being the first African American to shoot a Vogue cover in the magazine's 125 year history.

Images often inspire emotions to surface as the subconscious recognizes a compelling truth that holds our gaze.

An artist familiar with producing arresting images is Tyler Mitchell. This 27 year old native from Atlanta became the first black photographer to shoot the cover of Vogue. For this historic occurrence, he chose the perfect subject, Beyonce.

His ascent was never assured. While in elementary school, he picked up a camera and developed a proficiency for capturing images. To edit his work, he watched Youtube videos.

As Tyler matured, skateboarding culture fascinated him. An opportunity to travel to Cuba surfaced and he leveraged this jaunt to document the subculture of skateboarders. He turned that six week excursion into a 108 page book entitled El Paquete. To nurture and refine his approach, he attended New York University Tisch School for the Arts.

UPENDO BOOKS LTD

While there, he cultivated his skill for creating and editing short films. After graduating in 2017, Tyler refused to get an agent to further his career. Instead he posted his work on Instagram. This led to working with a litany of iconic companies such as: Marc Jacobs, JW Anderson, Converse, Nike, and Givenchy.

Now, his ultimate quest is to capture the "Black Utopian Vision". In his work, Tyler uses public spaces for a broader commentary about young black men. By focusing his "honest gaze" on people that are ignored, he draws more attention to their absence in any "mainstream" reflection of reality. He records the full spectrum of emotions in an unapologetic fashion through his work.

Rather than seeing representation as a question of morality, he posits it as a sports analogy.

"There are 12 soccer players on a field with one ball, and there's a goal, and all 12 can see the goal. Then they can quickly put the ball in the goal in two seconds. There's another way of operating where you have a group of inmates in prison who can all see the guard with the key, but they can't see each other, so they're not able to share information and figure out how to escape. Inclusion is simply the first one. It's just about sharing more information. It's about giving other people the visibility of saying Okay, here's the ball and the goal, and you can actually easily score."

Maintaining confidence as a young creative can be challenging.

Even Tyler struggles with the weight of various expectations, but he advises that young people practice their craft every day. All creatives in his mind need to express themselves to develop their individual sensibilities. For this to occur, maintaining an unwavering focus is necessary.

"If I'm not taking pictures, then I'm thinking about taking pictures".

Additionally, Tyler suggests that his peers ignore the emotions that arise from being praised or criticised.

Tyler is resolute in his view of capturing images.

"Photography being a full-time job

"When it comes to any type of feedback about your work, take it with a grain of salt"

is a hard thing to wrap your head around; there are so many aspects to it. There's the researching that goes on before, but then a shoot could just fall out of the sky right now. Ideas come and go, so you just have to be ready for when that comes and you have to be diligent, focused and work maybe even harder when you have all of this free time. Now that I live by myself in my own studio, I treat that as an important place for my work. I just keep working".

The above quote resonates with another creative, Tinu Akinwande, a 22 year old artist based out of Ottawa.

She captures images of the black community in its resplendent beauty.

At 22 years old, she envisioned and then worked to manifest a project entitled, "Black Women...Blossom". To her, all of the images that she captured celebrate resilience.

Building on the success of this project, she founded a conference entitled Black Brilliance. While developing her voice and further establishing her conference, she suffered a devastating personal loss. One of her best friends, Abel, was killed in a bus crash.

During this time, she attended to the needs of others until realising that her own mental health was suffering.

"When Abel died, I was the person who people came to. I got busy with school and work, and it didn't really give me much time to sit back and think. I didn't notice I was subconsciously going through a mental health battle of my own. While people were looking at me to console them, I didn't prioritise myself"

This resulted in an abiding depression that only seemed to wane after she found her creative voice. "I thought ... I have a camera and I can edit a bit, let me see if I can create a story of my triumphs and trials and see if I could help people."

Ultimately, Tilu dedicated her project to Abel. "Abel would have been very happy about this. He used to rock a big afro. We were supposed to take photos like this together."

As for her work, Tilu wants it to have a resonating effect. Morgan Hamilton-Kirk, the Founder of the Niche Ottawa Art Gallery, confirms the power of Tilu's work. "It's a spectacular portrayal of the Black woman's experience"

POETIC PROMISE

"Poetry is activism. You can *express yourself* in a way that pushes a movement forward"

Nyarae Francis is a 16 year old high school student from Inglewood, CA.

Her work focuses on community, academic inequality, mental health, the joys of life, family, gender and sexuality. She also touches on the black experience through the eyes of a young woman finding healing and growth through poetry.

In thinking about the impact and resonance of her work, she is reflective about the larger opportunity that exists.

Using pain as a fulcrum to initiate progress is an approach that INARI WILLIAMS, a 21 year old creative from Chicago embraces. She lost a close friend to gun violence during her junior year of high school. During the aftermath of this tragic event, she experienced a plethora of emotions.

Although this continues to be a source of trauma, she turned to poetry as a means of addressing her emotions. And by creating works of art, she provided an opportunity and a space for others with similar experiences to feel seen, heard, valued, and embraced.

ALORA YOUNG, a 19 year old from Tennessee supports this form of artistic service. She was the 2021 Youth Poet Laureate of the Southern United States. Her memoir, Walking Gentry Home celebrates not only the strength of her foremothers, but also acknowledges the transformative power that derives from honest acts of creation.

"I believe poetry is something that can cross any line, any border. We need to try to cross these lines and connect our world through the arts because we can make the world better."

THE I
WIT
YOU ~
LIC
WITH

IGHT
HIN
IS THE
HT
IN US

UPENDO BOOKS LTD

TELL my Story

Olivia VG Clarke tried to "fit in" but instead of losing herself, she wrote a book to help students like her find their own voice.

As a high school juniour in Columbus, Ohio, Olivia was at odds with her environment. She felt herself slipping away as she tried to replace her identity with one that was palatable to her peers. But Olivia noticed that in the process of wanting to be liked, she was compromising her true nature and preventing any type of honest expression from surfacing. She began to find this approach to interacting with others troubling.

Her voice lowers as she remembers that period of her life. "I spent a lot of time trying to mold myself and fix myself into this white standard that I saw in school. The girl who gets called pretty always has straight hair, she's blonde, she has blue eyes. I can't do that, but I can try to, you know, adjust the way I dress to look like her, just the way I straighten my hair to try to get it like hers and things like that, which was really damaging my self-esteem and my self-image in middle school."

Instead of hiding her struggle in shame, Olivia wrote a book entitled, *'Black Girl, White School: Thriving, Surviving, and No, You Can't Touch My Hair,'* to help other young black women reclaim and celebrate their identities.

In the process she experienced things that were unsettling to her such as the school staff mixing up the names of students of colour. Another incident that she covers in her book occurred in a space normally designed to nurture peace and serenity.

"One time I kept being racially profiled, but in yoga class. It was weird because it wasn't in a store. Sometimes store clerks think I'm going to steal something. I didn't expect it in PE"

UPENDO BOOKS LTD

SOMETIMES THE STORM IS INSIDE OF YOU.

HURRICANE SUMMER

Olivia's advice to others is to move forward with actualizing their efforts to make a positive difference.

"Don't wait for someone else to start the conversation, open the door and take the first step. You can do it, I believe in you"

This sentiment is shared by Yohann Kamto, an author from Cameroon. He made history by being the first fiction writer in his native land to publish a book at the ripe age of 17.

His mystery novel continues to be celebrated. While discussing the work he created, he advises his contemporaries to envision "an ending before commencing a novel. This ensures that you stay focussed on reaching a goal".

After being asked about some of the aspects he loved about the creative process, he chuckles. "Incorporating false clues was fun. But I had to be careful not to include too many of them".

Keeping readers engaged is something that has marked the work of Asha Bromfield. This 29 year old writer from Toronto finished her second novel which should be published in 2023.

Her first book, Hurricane Summer is described as a love letter to Jamaica. It follows the experiences of Tilla and explores the estranged relationship she has with her father.

The complexity of developing into a young woman and the tension that this creates, remains a topic fascinates Asha. She describes the inner conflicts that arise out of complex familial relationships.

"Tilla has grown up with a longing for her father. You always hear about girls having, quote-unquote, 'daddy issues' — but I wanted to show the longing that's created when you have the imprint of a really great father"

She is quick to illustrate the different roles that young women are expected to occupy without their explicit consent.

"As you move into your teens you're no longer loved and revered by your father because you're not this cute little girl anymore. It speaks to society and the way that we view young women, the way that we view sexual young women, how we value women and their virginity and how we shame girls when we feel they're, quote-unquote, 'promiscuous.'"

Like most authors, the work she

"Believe in your art, your voice, and your creativity. Not everyone will see your vision, but follow your truth"

created draws inspiration from her own life. The pain that she felt growing up with an estranged father found its way onto her pages.

"Distance creates a deep wound. That was something I had felt firsthand growing up. When you become a pre-teen or early teenager and you realise that the world looks at you a bit differently and you're no longer the cute little girl that you were before."

As for helping other young black women, Asha considers it an honour.

"It's a divine privilege to be able to represent for so many Black women out there. We deserve to be seen, held, recognized and, above all, loved. Because we are Love. We are worthy and so valuable. We are mystical and deeply magical. There are so many goddesses out there just waiting to wake up to their power. To come home to their ancestral truths. I feel so blessed to contribute to that narrative through my work. My only goal is to continue to create work that honours that and celebrates the divinity of Black and brown women all over the world. I also get so excited about more Caribbean representation because there is so much medicine/healing in the islands"

Asha is also quick to advise others to embrace all aspects of their journey.

"It's no secret that racism is insidious in the industry. But I think it's important to highlight that I really, really love being a Black woman. It takes so much softness and deep compassion to move through the world the way we do—and that's what Black women represent to me - Love. We are resilient but still so soft, loving and deserving. I take so much pride and joy in that. It's such a privilege for me to be a Black, Afro-Caribbean women in this incarnation and I celebrate that so deeply. I think a lot of us do, and that's important to highlight. It's a blessing to be a Black woman and I give thanks every day! I'm excited by the changes that are happening in the industry, and I look forward to changing the narrative around the truth of who we are, and our capacity to feel and heal ourselves"

All of these creatives demonstrate that great triumphs come from our greatest challenges.

Business

OUR FOUNDATION

At 22 years old, ZANDRA CUNNINGHAM'S cosmetic company is making millions, but her journey started after she was told «No»

It was an ordinary day but one that changed her life. She casually asked her father for a few dollars to purchase an item, but he refused. It was then that Zandra decided that she would never ask anyone for anything ever again.

As a 13 year old, she became the youngest person to ever graduate from The Allstate Minority and Women Entrepreneurial Program at the University at Buffalo School of Management.

While increasing her income is important, her underlying goal is to empower others. She teaches classes on entrepreneurship, advising youth and adults on how they can get started early building their dreams.

As a TEDx speaker, Zandra is a recognized entrepreneur in the Buffalo community and collaborations include Black Enterprise, NPR, Seventeen Magazine, Teen Boss, Girls Life Magazine, Teen Boss, Forbes, INC, USA TODAY, and Nickelodeon. The TODAY Show, Steve Harvey's Funderdome, The Harry Connick Jr. Show, Good Morning America, and ABC Nightline are also on the growing list.

Her recent features and collaborations include Black Enterprise, NPR, Seventeen Magazine, Teen Boss, Girls Life Magazine, Forbes, INC, USA TODAY, and Nickelodeon. The TODAY Show, Steve Harvey's Funderdome, Good Morning America, and ABC Nightline.

Zandra started her journey in business by mixing up lip balm in the kitchen at her house.

Today she has a GMP compliant manufacturing and distribution facility. As an eco-friendly social good company in Western New York, Zandra is committed to sustainable practices that prioritize sensitive skin types.

Her mission is to create high quality, fun + fresh products that smell amazing but don't have all the unnecessary yucky stuff + chemicals.

"We have the power to change not only our own lives, but those around us like our family and our community"

Zandra is also a philanthropist. She donates up to 10% of all net profits to support girls' education. She founded Day of the Girls Buffalo, an international movement. This girl-powered all expenses paid day for girls has one goal: to connect girls with their community, provide educational options and ideas.

Her advice to other young people is simple.

"Starting is the first step to greatness. Just start".

Building a community is something that also resonates with the leaders of Harlem Capital. This venture capital firm was founded in 2005 by Henri Pierre-Jacques and Jarrid Tingle after they noticed that minority owned companies were being overlooked by VC firms despite being viable businesses. To address this inequity, Henri and Jarrid sought to acquire knowledge so they could empower others. Henri earned his MBA from Harvard and Jarrid received his MBA from Wharton Business School. They met and decided to create a diversity-focused venture capital firm.

The goal of these young men was to invest in 1,000 diverse founders over the next 20 years. Their inaugural fund closed as an angel syndicate at $40 million. They now have $174 million in assets under management.

> "We have the power to change not only our own lives, but those around us like our family and our community"

Asked about the origins of his interest in business, Henri becomes whimsical. Broadly speaking, he first learned about making a profit in eighth grade after his mom introduced him to the stock market. She promised to double his allowance of $25 if he invested in the market. Being a smart child, he took a keen interest in learning about the rules to becoming wealthy.

Now, Harlem Capital has two venture funds. The first fund includes 23 companies that vary from e-commerce platforms to wellness brands. The second fund is comprised of 45 companies that are led by minority or women founders and are in the early seed stage.

With its second fund, Harlem Capital will also introduce "Culture Carry" — allowing Fund II founders to split 1% of the fund's carry. Fund I founders will also now have culture carry. The decision ensures all founders will benefit directly from each other's successes. This also aligns with Harlem Capital's mission to promote a stronger ecosystem of diverse founders.

"We are focused on building an institution and platform to support diverse founders for many generations. Fund II is one step closer to our mission, but we know the work and journey continues. We are excited to provide more capital and resources to even more diverse founders tackling unique problems,"

Fund II's limited partners ("LPs") include 14 world-class institutions, 4 global corporations, and 6 family offices. The firm is proud to have the support of 18 General Partners belonging to other investment funds, with 42% of Fund II's individual LPs being women or people of color.

The focus on empowering underserved communities is also supported by Arlan Hamilton, the Founder and Managing Partner of Backstage Capital.

At 28 years old, she also noticed that traditional venture capital firms were ignoring businesses that were led by people of colour. Although she didn't have any background in business, Arlan studied hard and reached out to mentors. Her efforts paid off.

To date, Arlan has helped over 200 companies become profitable.

"At Backstage, we invest in the very best founders who identify as women, People of Color, or LGBTQ. I personally identify as all three."

AFRICAN GENIUS

UPENDO BOOKS LTD

Ramarni Wilfred, a 19 year old from the UK holds an IQ of 162 which places him above Albert Einstein, Bill Gates, and Stephen Hawking.

His mother, Anthea Wilfred noticed that on one occasion while driving her son to the nursery,

"He was telling me about something he'd seen on the news, and it was a very political subject. Later on that afternoon, I saw the topic on the TV and I thought, my two-and-a-half-year-old has just been talking to me about this in the car. It was just bizarre."

Ramarni's incisive observations fell in line with his developmental leaps. He was able to read and write in preschool and at 10 years old, he wrote a theoretical paper on justice and won a plethora of prestigious awards.

This brought him to the attention of MENSA, an organisation noted for extending membership only to those possessing Iqs belonging to the top 2% of the population. After taking the MENSA test, Ramarni scored within the top 1% of the population.

"Success is about finding your thing and finding what you are very interested in learning about"

Ramarni is the youngest person to achieve this distinction to date. But to Ramarni's family, signs of his brilliance started very early.

HOW IS IQ MEASURED?

Some of the most widely used IQ tests include:

Wechsler Intelligence Scale for Children (WISC-V)

Wechsler Intelligence Scale for Adults (WAIS)

Stanford–Binet Intelligence Scale

Differential Ability Scales (DAS)

Peabody Individual Achievement Test

These tests are usually given by licensed psychologists and are divided into several sections.

The Wechsler Intelligence Scale, for example, contains 15 subtests. Each subtest measures a different aspect of IQ, such as math, language, reasoning, memory, and information processing speed. The results are then combined into one score called the IQ. The scores are also adjusted by age.

RISING IQS

Since the early 1900s, raw scores on IQ tests have largely increased in most parts of the world. This phenomenon is sometimes called the "Flynn effect" after the scientist who discovered it, James Flynn.

It's also important to remember that the concept of IQ and IQ tests were developed by Western Europeans according to their own cultural standards.

It's still unclear whether IQ can accurately measure intelligence in people with completely different social structures, cultures, beliefs, and ways of thinking.

On top of this, it's clear that environmental factors play a huge role in average IQ. Factors that have been positively associated with higher IQ scores include: happiness, not pain or mindless self-indulgence, is the proof of your moral integrity, since it is the proof and the result of your loyalty to the achievement of your values.

HOW DOES RAMARNI STAY HUMBLE?

After receiving his IQ score, he didn't take on a different identity.

Instead, he continued to enjoy the activities that brought him joy and strengthened the connection with his family and friends. These activities include reading comic books and playing games.

E N A B L E
COURAGE

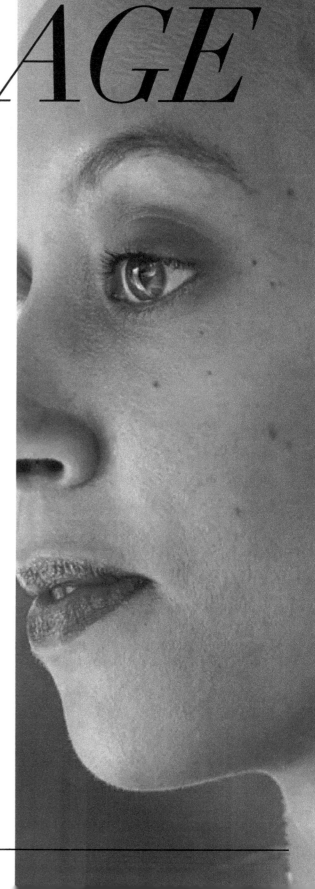

Haben Girma proves that having a disability doesn't prevent anyone from living a full and exciting life. She like many others are using their gifts to help the disabled community feel more seen, heard, accepted, and embraced.

As a 19 year old student at Lewis & Clark College in Portland, OR, Haben Girma had an experience that forever altered the course of her life. That day progressed like any other. She woke up, attended classes, and studied for tests. By lunchtime she had worked up a strong appetite.

Haben went to the cafeteria to satiate her hunger. Before she ordered, she requested a menu in braille from the manager.

Unfortunately, he refused to give her one.

Rather than protest, Haben tolerated consuming meals without any idea of their ingredients. This was troubling given that she was a vegetarian. Finally, Haben had reached her threshold for suffering in silence. She did some research and discovered that under the Americans with Disabilities Act , her school was bound by law to provide a legible menu for all students.

Without any hesitation, she articulated this point to the cafeteria manager and he promptly began sending her emails with menu items.

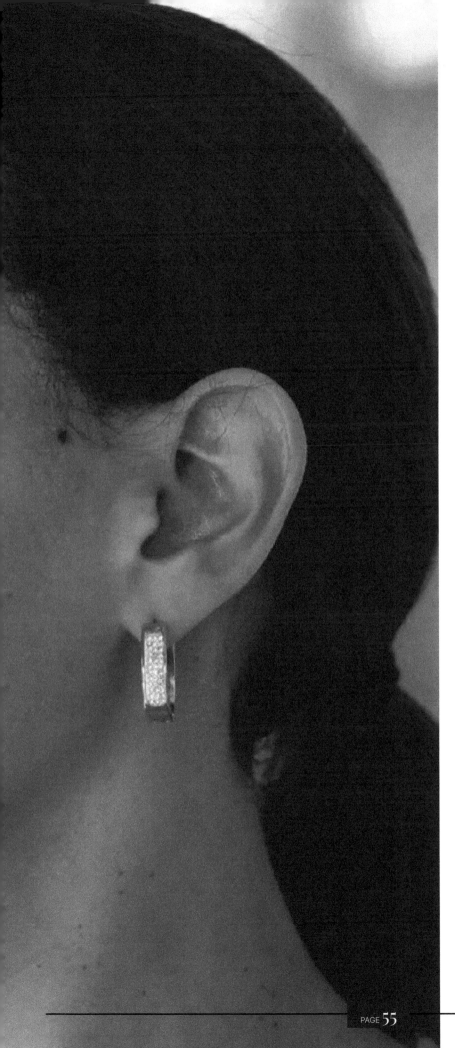

The next year another blind student arrived to find an accessible menu. Knowing that she had affected change on her campus inspired Haben to dedicate her life to serving those with disabilities. This mission led her to Harvard Law School. While there, she distinguished herself by becoming the first deaf / blind student to receive a degree from this venerable institution. Her time at Harvard, however, was fraught with challenges.

"The school didn't know exactly which accommodations I needed. Neither did I. Doing law school deaf-blind was new to me, too. We engaged in an interactive process. We tried different strategies until we found the right solutions. I passed all my classes, even earning several honours,"

After being asked about her process for staying focused despite these challenges, Haben is reflective.

"My personal experience with discrimination, as well as those I heard from others, sparked my desire to develop my advocacy skills. In my final year, I was honored with a Skadden Fellowship, one of the most prestigious fellowships in the legal field. The Skadden Foundation provided two years of financial support for my work to increase access to digital reading services for blind students"

Being the exceptional person that she is, Haben also developed a device that allowed her to communicate with others. Rather than reading lips, she instructs those wanting to speak with her to type out their messages on a wireless keyboard. It transmits the communication to another device that translates the message into braille. Haben reads the message and then responds by speaking to the person.

Her accomplishments earned her the honour of being named Whitehouse Champion of Change by President Barack Obama. To relax, Haben surfs, salsa dances, climbs icebergs, and bullfights.

"As a disabled black woman, lots of stories say my life doesn't matter. I had to learn to resist them"

BLACK THEATRE MATTERS

DRAMATIC TURN

More young playwrights are finding their voices.

Futuma Adar, a playwright from Toronto developed a musical entitled Dixon Road after noting the lack of diversity within the Canadian theatre.

"When something doesn't exist you kind of just have to make it".

Her play, Dixon Road focuses on the journey of a Somali family that immigrated to Canada in 1991 to escape a civil war.

While many would be correct to assume that this play deals with themes of transience and belonging, at the heart of the piece is the relationship between a father and daughter. Each seeks to retain their identity while adjusting to a new culture.

"It's a dynamic of what it means to take care of each other, to listen to each other, to find each other".

It is also difficult to ignore the issue of progress given that the father, who is a documentarian in the play, realises that he will not be able to achieve the same level of success as he did in Somalia. While this revelation surfaces, his daughter is discovering a plethora of opportunities she wouldn't have enjoyed in the land of her birth. This tension creates an engaging narrative that allows the audience to reflect on their own sacrifices despite their ethnic backgrounds.

The play holds a close resemblance to reality given that Futuma's family also fled and settled in Canada.

"I hope [others] find themselves in the story of what a lot of diasporic kids go through, which involves the sacrifices our parents made for us"

Futuma's father, Mohamed earned asylum in Canada and then sent for his family. At that time, their community on Dixon Road was small. As more families from Somalia arrived, Futuma's father became their guide. He helped them get settled and navigate the city. The community that developed was tight knitted given that they were fleeing a civil war. "It was important to be able to create a community in Canada that they could call home"

The desire to make others feel seen in a theatrical space resonates with Jackie Sibblies Drury.

She is a Brooklyn native whose work, Fairview earned her a Pulitzer.

In the first act, a happy, comfortable black family depicted in sitcoms is introduced.

In the second act, the same scenes that occurred in the first act are replayed but an audio overlay of four white people debating race is added.

To heighten the emotional impact of the piece, audience members that identify as white are invited on stage.

This unexpected occurrence often garners Jackie the most praise.

Despite the confidence she exudes in her work, Jackie's creative process was riddled with self-doubt.

In describing the journey to complete the play, she expresses a refreshing vulnerability.

"There were so many nervous tears and false starts and the panic that if I can't figure out this play, I'm not going to graduate. I chewed on it, and chewed on it, and chewed on it. But there was an earnest desire to explore both the story and also my right to tell it, and to be very rigorous about that".

Her passion for the theatre and the intricate nature of manifesting a compelling narrative drove her forward until the piece was complete. The collaborative nature of bringing a play to its feet inspired Jackie.

"Theatre is so difficult, there are so many moving parts. As a writer I have control over the words, but not really any control over what the whole show ends up meaning, and so it feels good to be able to work with people I trust and who have integrity, intellect and, yes, also silliness. It feels rare to me".

> "I find it inspiring that a lot of different people can come into a room and focus on one goal"

As far as craft, her advice to other writers is to explore the layers of every character. She also encourages creatives to develop nuance as a way to cultivate depth.

"To write about anything, you have to declare something and I find that very hard to do. I do very much feel: 'Is my blue the same blue as your blue?' I have that about everything. I think it's very hard to say Jamaican people are like this, or black people are like this, or white people are like this. That's part of my attraction to writing through things in theatre, because in [the character] Mary Seacole, for example, we have three different white women who play different versions of themselves, but they also are able to refract and prismatically create something that's more complicated than just one white woman is".

WHAT IS THE VALUE OF THEATRE IN THE MODERN AGE?

Jackie offers a resolute response.

"It sounds incredibly Pollyannaish, but I do think a big part of theatre is reminding people of their own humanity, in a complicated way. It's to use empathy to think through the way that our society functions"

WHAT IS THE LEGACY OF YOUR WORK?

Futuma notes that she wants her work to create joy.

"I will always remember Dixon Rd. as the first place to welcome my family and create a legacy of what Little Mogadishu becomes"

Jackie also wants to inspire others.

Interview

GREEN PANTHER

Wanjiku "Wawa" Gatheru is the first black person to receive the Rhodes, Truman, and Udall Scholarships in succession. Her next goal? Solve our climate crisis.

As a Graduate Student at Oxford University her focus is studying Environmental Governance.

"Climate change, as devastating as it is, presents us with an opportunity to create a just future for all of us"

WHAT WAS WANJIKU'S FIRST EXPERIENCE WITH THE CLIMATE CHANGE MOVEMENT?

At 15, she took an environmental science class and her teacher integrated environmental justice into the curriculum. It was then she realised that social justice issues - racial justice, gender justice, sexual justice, ect. had everything to do with the environment.

This realisation inspired her to view the climate crisis and the environmental movement as a narrative.

"It was a story — actually, a saga of heartbreak and loss, of millions of people that are being relocated, of climate refugees who are seeing their homelands surrender to the sea. We're seeing people experiencing famine in ways that they'd never seen before, and who are questioning the ways that they can live and have livable futures. We're seeing children go out and strike on streets"

HOW CAN OTHER YOUNG PEOPLE GET MORE INVOLVED IN THE MOVEMENT?

Wanjiku's voice rises with excitement. In her opinion, aligning activism with the important things in her life has made a significant difference. She advises others to do the same. In her estimation, coupling the issues that someone holds dear with the cause that they want to serve would not only bolster their commitment to serve, but would also fuel their passion for making a positive difference.

As an example, if a young person wanted to help an organisation eradicate illiteracy, they could imagine a loved one being forced to live in destitution based on their inability to read.

For Wanjiku, she remains committed to the environmental movement. The seeds of her alliance with it were germinated in the fields owned by many of her relatives in Kenya. On it, Wanjiku's family tilled the land from generation to generation.

The food that she consumed throughout her childhood was delivered by relatives cultivating nutrients on their family plot.

Her earliest memories were spent gardening with her mom and grandmother. They taught her the importance of reciprocity and developed her perpetual concern for the planet. However, it was not until she reached high school that she considered herself an "environmentalist". Up until then, she felt disconnected from the mainstream depictions of environmentalism and the issues that she cared the most about.

WHAT WAS WANJIKU'S JOURNEY?

After spending a year in Buriram, Thailand as a Kennedy-Lugar Youth Exchange and Study (YES) Scholar of the United States Department of State, Wanjuku returned to study environmental science and policy at the University of Connecticut. As a budding academic, her goal was to contribute to intersectional environmental scholarship.

Understanding food insecurity as being a climate issue, she co-founded the UConn Access to Food Effort (UCAFE). She soon created and distributed the first campus-wide food insecurity survey at any public college in the state.

She served as a lead organizer in Connecticut's first Youth Climate Lobby Day, where over 100+ young people from around the state lobbied state legislatures to support environmental legislation.

Her leadership helped spark a resurgence of environmental activism at the University of Connecticut. There, she guided a movement that pushed for UConn to become the first public university in the country to implement an environmental literacy general education requirement. It was such a successful initiative that she earned a place as a United Nations Global Health Fellow. As the University's first Black student body vice president, she was selected by the University President as student co-chair of the University-wide Metanoia, where she led a steering committee of 20 faculty members, other staff, and administrators. In this position, she helped to coordinate various events and workshops across UConn's undergraduate and graduate programming.

HOW IS WANJIKU MAKING A DIFFERENCE NOW?

She founded Black Girl Environmentalist, a nonprofit committed to addressing the pathway and retention problems in environmental science and advocacy for Black girls, Black women and Black non-binary people. In this space, Wanjiku amplifies the voices of those wanting to improve society as well as the environment.

"This movement is not one person, or one group. This movement is all of us and we need to make sure we value those who are disproportionately affected by this crisis. And allow those who are affected to lead"

Article

CLEAR SIGN

Roy Allela invented "smart" gloves to help his deaf niece communicate with the rest of their family. Now, his creation is bringing together millions around the globe.

Roy's incredible invention converts the movements of sign language into audio speech. The idea for these gloves surfaced while Roy watched in agony as his niece attempted to communicate with members of their family. Her inability to understand others and be understood broke his heart. That day he promised her that she never would feel isolated again.

In describing the way in which his gloves work, Roy is bound by emotion. "My niece pairs them to her phone or mine, then starts signing and I'm able to understand what she's saying"

Roy knew that his invention could be improved so he sought out reviewers from a special needs school. One of the most helpful suggestions was altering the translation speed. Just as people speak at varying rates, people also sign at different speeds.

Roy integrated this function into the mobile application for his smart gloves. Now, users can pick their native language, gender, and even have the ability to control the

pitch of vocalisation during their conversations.Even though all of these functions are impressive on their own, the accuracy of the gloves are now over 93%.

Being a dedicated engineer, Roy wanted to improve his smart gloves so he decided to customise them as a way of reflecting the personalities of each owner. Now, users can pick almost any design for their gloves.

His incredible invention earned Roy an award from The American Society of Mechanical Engineers. Like any true innovator, Roy reinvested the prize money into improving the translation as well as the vocal prediction component of his smart gloves.

In describing the inspiration behind continuing to improve his invention, he takes a moment to respond.

"I was trying to envision how my niece's life would be if she had the same opportunities as everyone else as far as education, employment, and all aspects of life are concerned".

He takes a breath before continuing.

"The general public in Kenya doesn't understand sign language, so when she goes out, she always needs a translator. Over the long term that type of dependency is crippling. It would plague or impair her progress in life. That's the reason I've really strived to develop this audio translator project to completion."

The desire to help others continues to inspire BETELHEM DESSIE. At 23 years old, this Ethiopian entrepreneur is working to equip girls with the skills they need to work in the burgeoning tech sector in Ethiopia. Although her days are filled with joy, her emergence on the tech scene was borne out of pain.

"Freedom to do something leads to accomplishment and that accomplishment drives excitement"

At 9 years old, her father refused to celebrate her birthday.

That day, Betelhem promised herself to become a tech entrepreneur so that she would have the means to fund her own celebrations. She began to learn about computer engineering with the help of Google. She also relied on borrowed books from local Universities.

After spending countless hours studying, Betelhem began to apply her knowledge. It took some time but she began earning income from video editing and installing cellphone software. As her skills became more proficient, news spread. Soon, she was being interviewed by local news stations.

Her reputation drew the attention of the Prime Minister of Ethiopia, Meles Zenawi. He invited her to move to the capital, Addis Ababa with her immediate family.

At ten years old, she was working on confidential projects for the government. Rather than resting on her laurels, Betelhem completed her tasks and found time to develop and copyright four software programs, including a digital library that she created in grade 10. The program helps schools with limited internet connectivity to access the resources that their students need to learn. Betelhem also invented an app that enabled the government to track irrigation systems by mapping rivers and made it open source - any agricultural professional with a smartphone can contribute to the app.

"In Africa we have a lot of young people. If we train the young generation in tech, we'll build something everlasting".

MUSE on *Zen*

Tabay Atkins is America's youngest Certified Yoga Teacher. His journey began after his mother got cancer. He was six years old.

Tabay shaved his head as his mother, Sahel began to lose her own hair after being diagnosed with stage 3 cancer.

During this time, he remembered the toll that chemotherapy treatments had on his mother's body. "It broke her down physically and emotionally". After his mother was in remission, she discovered yoga. Even though Sahel could barely walk, her friend asked her to take a 200 hour yoga teaching course. Despite her frailty, Sahel accepted the invitation and noticed that her yoga practice was making her stronger. "I didn't have the heaviness that cancer brings".

Inspired by his mother's burgeoning recovery, Tabay committed himself to learning yoga. His focus was so unwavering that while his friends played and collected toys, Tabay, at 10 years old, enrolled in an intensive yoga course. He worked hard to finish the requirements and then graduated to complete different types of specialisations.

Now, at 16 years old, Tabay teaches classes three days a week at Sahel's studio, Care4Yoga, and donates his earnings to cancer patients. Tabay's accomplishments have garnered international attention and he is routinely invited to lead sessions in various countries such as France, Australia, and Mexico. Many of his adult students often underestimate Tabay's abilities until they finish his class.

"My sixth-grade English teacher took one of my classes — she has been doing yoga for 19 years — and she said my class was the best one she ever took".

UPENDO BOOKS LTD

Even though his accomplishments are impressive, Tabay notes that he is only at the beginning stage of his journey of serving others.

"I want to try to open up as many studios as I can and spread the yoga word. Yoga helps in a lot of ways so I want to teach yoga to anyone and everyone I can."

Brandon Dawson - Jarvis is another practitioner that experienced the healing effects of a sustained yoga practice.

As a young man in Quebec, he spent three and a half years behind bars. Instead of it being a rehabilitating experience, it exacerbated his emotional struggles.

"The best way to create change is to stop theorizing and start doing"

"I came out of prison in a worse state than when I went in. I had PTSD. I was having nightmares. The anger that I felt before turned into rage."

Afraid that Brandon would commit another crime, someone close to him suggested yoga.

At first, Brandon laughed at the idea. "It was ridiculous". Despite his initial misgivings, Brandon now runs a healthcare business called Grove

Campus. This retreat offers yoga classes, apparel, and mats online. Thinking back on his childhood, Brandon credits yoga with providing the emotional stability that he didn't have as a child.

"My parents had me at a very young age, so they didn't really have all of the emotional tools to navigate parenthood"

Instead of anger, Brandon now feels compassion for himself and his family. He credits yoga for his peaceful disposition. Grove Campus, the wellness business that he runs offers classes and pay what you can sessions.

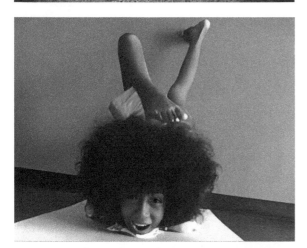

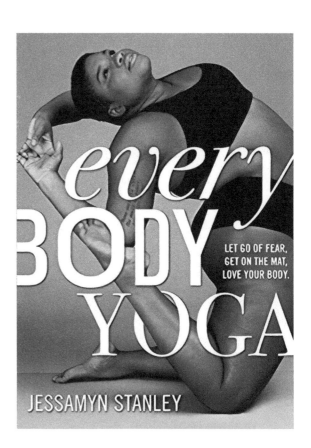

every
BODY
YOGA

LET GO OF FEAR,
GET ON THE MAT,
LOVE YOUR BODY.

JESSAMYN STANLEY

Graphic Tale

Taylor K Shaw wanted to hire black women animators. She couldn't find any, so she became the youngest CEO in the animation industry

Before Taylor made history, she was working on a project. For this series, she wanted her experiences as a black woman living in Chicago to be reflected. The only problem was she couldn't find one animator that was a black woman.

"In animation, you don't really see any women at all. You see a few white women, very few women of colour, and hardly any black women at all. What we're doing [here] is transforming the media landscape and making sure that women of color are included in this space"

She envisioned her platform now known as the Black Women Animate - (BWA). In her mind, it would be a community based endeavour that would also heighten the visibility of talented yet overlooked professionals.

To quantify the problem of representational lack, Taylor completed extensive research to uncover racial disparities in animation. She wasn't able to find much data. Her task was made even more difficult by the fact that inequitable representation wasn't only confined to race.

"These demographics show women in animation, yes, and they show that most university animation programs are mostly women. But who is getting these jobs? White males. Men are getting the jobs; women are not"

To gain a more precise perspective, Taylor adopted an incremental approach.

"Our goal is to get some studies out there that show the demographics of women of colour in the industry, but you won't find the numbers broken down because they don't exist. The fact that there aren't any numbers proves that there are very few, if any, black women, and if there are we need them to be a part of our collective".

> ## "We're breaking down walls, creating access, building bridges, and getting people meaningful work they love."

Prior to becoming an animator, Taylor was a journalist. She describes the pivot from it to animation as a labour of love.

"Not to sound disillusioned but the reason that I left journalism was because I didn't feel it was the best platform to make a difference".

To make the impact that she wanted, Taylor created her organization, Black Women Animate in 2017.

It is the first and only company specifically for black women and is delineated by tiers.

The VIP Collective Membership allows its members to be represented by the talent agency; a Collective Membership gives members the opportunity to receive training and development; and a Youth Membership is available for ages 10–18.

In describing the ambitions of the collective, Taylor remains focussed.

"Our goal is to, one, help members get the jobs they want, and, two, build a community for them. That's where they fit in. We're training and developing, getting their skills up, honing them, and then our goal is to funnel them into these major animation studios and media companies. For the talent agency, we represent them, and we produce work, animation, and motion graphics for different clients"

Taylor is also aware of the power of generating engaging content.

"For our original content, we have an animated series that we're pitching. That's going really well. We actually have two animated series right now in our original content vault and the potential for a feature film, which is super exciting. We're talking to many studios about that and that's exciting.

Then we're building a community for them [our members]".

On reflecting on the underlying mandate of Black Women Animate, Taylor's voice lowers.

"It is to become the company that people in the world of animation come to and say, 'Yo, can you guys teach us how to transform what diversity and inclusion looks like for us? Because we need the help because we want to produce the most purposeful content that really resonates with our viewers. Or we want to create content to reach this audience'".

Taylor believes that as more companies awaken to the need for more equitable representation, the more she has to be mindful of the partnerships she forms.

One of the most important aspects of working with anyone remains identifying their intentions. For companies only concerned with "looking good", Taylor is quick to dismiss them.

"We were building our movement before the 'awakening' and we'll continue to build it".

After being asked about the ways that corporations can communicate their commitment to working with organisations like Black Women Animate, Taylor smiles.

"It's time for media companies to start reaching out to all people that are out there, and it's time for them to do that in a conscious way, and you can only do that consciously by hiring and incorporating the narratives of all people. We're starting here with women of color — with black women. I'm so excited about it, but it's challenging work. It's necessary work"

As for the reasoning behind the glaring lack of black women in the field of animation, Taylor is expressive.

"I think partially this [equitable representation] hasn't been addressed because people assume that everything is fair across the board. It's like oh,...open opportunities for all. We all have to

actively do our part to make sure that representation is there. For me, storytelling is at the center of all of the work because everyone deserves liberty and the pursuit of happiness".

Taylor also advises that everyone, and young people especially get comfortable communicating 'uncomfortable' emotions.

This doesn't mean raising your voice or being confrontational, but respectfully yet assertively addressing an incident or comment that is insensitive.

She uses her own experience as an example.

"At my previous workplace, there have been times that I didn't say anything for a while and things got so bad because I didn't communicate. So I think that learning how to stand up for ourselves is important"

We recommend *Non-Violent Communication* by Marshall Rosenburg to help guide your approach to these talks.

Gabrielle Turnquest passed the UK bar at only 18 years old. This makes her the youngest person to achieve this distinction. Many call it a byproduct of her IQ, she disagrees.

JUR

INJUSTICE ANYWHERE IS A THREAT TO JUSTICE EVERYWHERE.

MARTIN LUTHER KING JR

Understanding Gabrielle's achievements require you to appreciate the magnitude of her work ethic and tenacity.

Her mother, Patrice Smith Bullard even tested Gabrielle and found out that she wasn't "gifted".

She notes that Gabrielle had other aptitudes.

"For me to say I recognized she was a genius? No. But Gabrielle was prepared to do the work and was very vigilant. She was serious about her work, but always found time to play"

HOW DID HER MOTHER HELP GABRIELLE EXCEL?

Patrice created a curriculum that allowed Gabrielle and her siblings to fast track their academic experience.

"At that time, homeschooling was not as accepted. I created a curriculum. I gave what the Sunshine State Standards would be, and I was able to give her two years of schooling in one academic year."

In describing her path to becoming a barrister, a smile spreads across Gabrielle's face.

"While I come from a family of lawyers, I didn't consider law as a career until I was a postgraduate. I started my undergraduate degree at the age of 14, but I studied with my own age group until I was about eight or nine. I was doing a lot of traveling and ended up moving back to the Bahamas where I was homeschooled for a while. During that period I was able to accelerate my studies, so by the time I got back to traditional schooling, I was around two years ahead of everyone else I was at school with. Since then, I have never fallen behind".

Even though she was studying online, Gabrielle did attend traditional classes for two years.

After high school, she attended a local community college and then transferred to Liberty University in Virginia. Instead of attending classes in person she opted for online courses while pursuing her Bachelor's Degree in the Science of Psychology.

After receiving this degree, Gabrielle began to think about graduate studies. She had always grown up discussing the law, however, being accepted into law school was difficult.

> "I want to urge other young persons to chase their dreams. Don't be afraid to start early!"

She applied and was accepted into the University of Law in London. Gabrielle was ecstatic, but her joy would soon be extinguished. The school rescinded their offer due to the fact that Gabrielle was not yet 18 years old.

"It took a lot of fighting and even transferring guardianship to my sister for the next year and a half so that my application could be reconsidered."

Rather than viewing her academic life as lacking excitement, Gabrielle views her journey as an enriching experience.

"I don't feel I have missed out on university life. I had my fair share

of wild nights out while in London in the last few months. I turned 18 in December before passing my bar exam so I had six or seven months of being legal in a foreign country. So, I definitely got that student experience at the tail-end of my academic career. I am still young and have time now to catch up on those experiences. I don't think I have missed out on anything, I have just decided to do it at a different time in my life. I will be able to get a lot more partying in once I actually don't have the worries of waking up and going to class."

GIVEN GABRIELLE'S YOUTH, HOW DO OTHER LAWYERS TREAT HER?

Before responding she laughs.

"The general reaction to my age has been shock. There is an initial disbelief but then people get used to it. It's not one of those things where people have come up to me constantly asking about it. Most people just assume that I am older anyway. Apart from being surprised, there has been very little negative feedback and no one has suggested my young age could be my downfall."

Her advice to her peers is to remain hopeful and focused.

"I don't think that my story should be used to show what just young people can do but what all people can do with hard work and determination. I am very grateful to all those who believed in me and hope that me sharing my story could persuade others to follow their dreams despite the challenges"

WHAT IS GABRIELLE'S ULTIMATE GOAL?

Rather than practice law in the UK, she will return to the US and chase her dream of becoming a fashion lawyer.

BUILDING BLOCKS

At 22 years old, Kimberly Dowdell graduated with a Bachelor of Architecture from Cornell University. Now, she is making history as the first black woman President of the American Institute of Architecture. She will serve as their leader in 2024. In describing the impact of this honour on her life, Kimberly is reflective.

> "We have to think about how to responsibly bring all these people together and what can we do to bring peace and harmony?"

"As the 295th living Black woman to earn an architectural license in the US, I am keen to help young women and people of colour"

HOW DID KIMBERLY GET STARTED IN ARCHITECTURE?

Her journey toward a career in architecture began in elementary school.

"My teacher gave us a shoebox and invited our class to make an apartment in it. I thought it was an interesting introduction to the power that is design"

Even back then Kimberly wasn't afraid of articulating her preferences. Although her discussions weren't as measured as they are now.

Her laughter rises describing the contentious interactions during her grade school group projects. She concedes that creative differences surfaced.

'The bed should go here! No, here! This is what carpet I want!'

As a more mature student, Kimberly recalls a trip she took to Detroit that sparked her desire to become an architect.

"I remember I was in downtown Detroit, which, in the early '90's, was a ghost of its former self - a lot of beautiful buildings that were built in Detroit's heyday were boarded up and not activated, and there wasn't a lot of street activity. I remember thinking, if architects work in space, then maybe I should become an architect and help to reactivate the buildings. I later realised, that's not how any of this works".

This experience taught her a valuable lesson about the importance of a collective.

"I learned that architecture involves the government, developers, contractors, engineers, etc. After I got licensed, I got a Master's of Public Administration degree. People will sometimes ask, 'Why would you study government when you are an architect?' Buildings are a part of the public realm. I felt like there are a lot of policies that inform how we interact with the built environment - what can be developed where, how high, what incentives do people get to do certain things – but that aren't developers. We're part of a larger team"

To young professionals following their passion, she only has one piece of advice.

"Find a mentor. It's really the secret to success. Not just mentorship, but relationship building in general. Even peer-to-peer, being a sounding board to people is important. No one has all the answers, but if you have a problem and you source solutions from a wider variety of people, you'll be able to make a stronger decision because of the diversity of thought that's gone into counseling you".

After being asked about her overall mission, Kimberly is quick to point out the importance of leveraging development and government capabilities. Kimberly admits that personalities sometimes clash but she views these interactions as opportunities to learn.

"When I was working with Maurice Cox in Detroit, he would sit down with the developer and say 'You can't build this here, because this doesn't respond to the context.' He used to be an architecture professor, so he would roll out trace paper, sit with the developer's architect, and say 'This is a better way to resolve this.'. There's so much happening within City Hall that shapes how we all interact with the built environment. Decisions are made with that sensitivity, which counterbalances the desire for profit on the developer side".

WHAT CHALLENGES DOES KIMBERLY CONTINUE TO FACE?

"Figuring out how I want to spend my time is somewhat of a challenge - finding the time to both deal with diversity issues, and also be a professional and advance that aspect

of my career. I'm passionate about urban revitalization, particularly rust belt cities, and places that have a rich history but have been disinvested. How do we reactivate these buildings with people and vibrant businesses? Ultimately, my professional mission is to improve the quality of life for people living in cities.

There is work to be done with the institutions and organisations that produce the people who shape the built environment. The programs that I'm looking to put in place now, if done well, can have a major impact on diversifying the profession".

HOW DOES KIMBERLY BUILD A SUPPORTIVE COMMUNITY?

She assists others without expectation of reciprocity and asks for help as she needs it. This is something she advises everyone to do despite their profession.

Article

FACE VALUE

Michael Oliver was accused of larceny after a facial recognition program identified him as an assailant. He was innocent yet remained under surveillance

One of the most troubling aspects of facial recognition technology is our inability to opt out of its pervasive gaze. Many are concerned that even though they are law abiding citizens, a technical error could upend their lives.

Michael Oliver can attest to this fact. He was falsely accused of larceny for allegedly reaching into a teacher's car, grabbing her cell phone, and breaking it.

A facial recognition system identified him as the guilty party even though a quick glance at the photo evidence would have easily exonerated him. The true culprit bore no resemblance to Michael given that the real assailant had no visible tattoos, a rounder face and darker skin.

Despite this glaring difference, the Detroit police moved forward with their investigation of Michael. He was brought in and put in a lineup.

The teacher that had their phone damaged then identified Michael.

WHY WAS MICHAEL CHARGED IN THE FIRST PLACE?

The police took an image that they garnered from a cellphone video and sent it through their facial recognition system.

> "I lost my job and my car; my whole life had to be put on hold... That technology shouldn't be used by police"

It was then that the system identified Michael. In court, the investigating officers admitted that they never interviewed anyone else that appeared in the same video.

It was also strange that Michael's case wasn't investigated by any supervisors in the prosecutor's office prior to his being charged. Protocol dictated that supervisors reviewed all evidence in facial recognition cases before a decision to charge anyone was reached.

After the evidence was reviewed in court, Michael's case was dismissed immediately.

HOW HAVE THINGS CHANGED SINCE MICHAEL'S CASE?

Now, all cases involving facial recognition have to be admitted to the highest ranking person in the prosecutor's office rather than any supervisor before any charges are issued. The new oversight measure will be triggered during the warrant charging phase, but before preliminary examinations.

This step is repeated after the case is referred to a Circut Court.

WHAT TYPE OF RECOURSE DID MICHAEL EXPERIENCE?

The police apologized but haven't done anything to address the ramifications that Michael suffered during this entire ordeal.

Michael grows silent and then shakes his head.

"I lost my job and my car; my whole life had to be put on hold. That technology shouldn't be used by police."

Studies have shown that computer algorithms have trouble identifying human faces, particularly those that are people of colour.

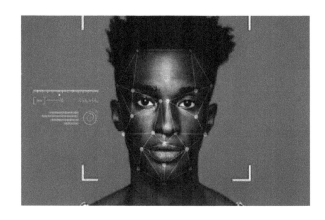

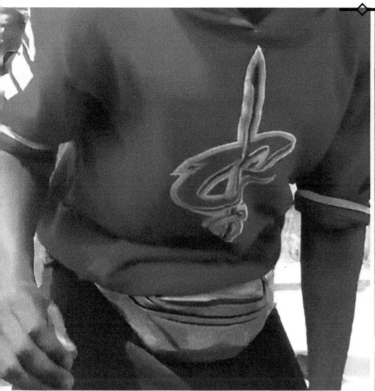
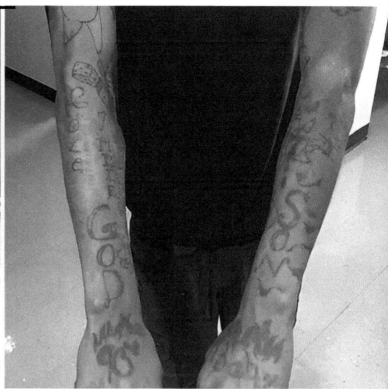

The landmark 2018 study, the "Gender Shades" project exposed divergent errors with the technology. During this project subjects were separated into four groups: dark-skinned males, darker-skinned females, lighter-skinned females, and lighter-skinned males.

All three algorithms performed the worst on darker-skinned females, with error rates up to 34% higher than for lighter-skinned males.

An independent assessment by the National Institute of Standards and Technology (NIST) has confirmed these studies, finding that face recognition technologies across 189 algorithms are the least accurate on women of color.

WHY ARE PEOPLE WORRIED ABOUT FACIAL RECOGNITION?

Many are troubled given that the technology that drives facial recognition software brings to mind the " lantern laws" that existed in New York during the 18th century. These troubling codes forced enslaved people to carry lanterns in the evening so that they would be publically visible. If facial recognition software continues to be applied unequally, some believe that it would be used to unfairly target certain areas while ignoring others. For those quick to deny the possibility of this occurrence, they need to only look at the impact of Project Greenlight (PGL). This "model" surveillance program used high-definition cameras throughout the city of Detroit. The data, which streams directly to Detroit PD, could be tested for face recognition against criminal databases, a driver's license, and state ID photos. One should note that almost every Michigan resident is in this system.

Some may argue that it is a necessary measure to keep everyone safe, but PGL stations are not distributed equally. Heightened surveillance correlates with majority-Black areas, avoiding White and Asian enclaves. A critical analysis noted that this program also had wider and more dangerous ramifications of simply being targeted. It was also discovered that surveillance and data collection were deeply connected to the diversion of public benefits, insecure housing, loss of employment opportunities, and policing leading to the criminilization of various community members.

If programs like this continue, it could lead to perpetuating racial inequality.

HOW CAN WE DEVELOP A MORE EQUITABLE FACIAL RECOGNITION SYSTEM?

First, algorithms can train on diverse and representative datasets, as standard training databases are predominantly White and male.

Second, establishing standards of image quality to run face recognition, and improving the settings for photographing Black subjects. Also, using intersecting identities (ex. young, darker-skinned, female) and working with organisations such as NIST and other independent entities may help to more accurately identify people of interest.

Michael's lawyer notes that facial recognition "has to stop until the science gets better".

NEW MONEY

Africa is leading the way in crypto markets. At the forefront are young people transforming the landscape of fungible tokens

A couple of Nigerian visionaries, Michael Adeyeri and Moyo Sodipo started a crypto company named Busha.

It raised $4.2 million in a seed round led by Jump Capital. Cadenza Ventures, Blockwall Capital, CMT Digital, Greenhouse Capital, and Raba Capital also took part in the round.

Michael and Moyo plan to reinvest the funds into product development, grow their company within Nigeria, and also expand into other African countries such as Ghana, and Kenya.

To become successful, Moyo and Michael focussed on serving their primary market.

UPENDO BOOKS LTD

❝ **O**ur approach while building has always been about customer obsession. We pay so much attention to what our customers want rather than what our competitors are doing"

This outlook helped Michael and Moyo build trust among those that they were serving.

Michael builds on Moyo's point about the growth that followed after serving the needs of their clients.

"We quickly realized that we were acquiring more customers through referrals just because we were delivering the exact kind of services that they wanted"

For those interested in entering the crypto market, Michael and Moyo advise you to focus on ease of use.

As an example, Michael and Moyo made their services even more attractive by mirroring the traditional Nigerian financial experience on their platform.

This meant offering real time communication that was available twenty four hours a day. Although this was a difficult task to implement, differentiated them immediately and allowed Busha to expand their customer base.

By becoming the first company to provide round the clock withdrawals as well as live chat, Bush proved that Nigeria could support a crypto market.

WHAT DO MICHAEL AND MOYO FOCUS ON DAY TO DAY?

Connecting with their clients is still very important to them. This is the primary focus of Moyo's role.

"We seek to create a crypto driven economy where there's fairness, transparency and access"

"My day to day involves connecting the support and marketing teams with the engineering team to make sure that every piece of feedback that I filter from customers is being implemented"

HOW ARE MICHAEL AND MOYO EXPANDING THEIR BUSINESS?

They are forming partnerships with well respected merchants so that their customers have more options and spend more time on their platform.

"We are working with SureGifts. Now, our customers can spend crypto across their merchant network. This includes Spart, Shoprite, and Jumia".

WHAT ARE MICHAEL AND MOYO'S NEXT STEPS?

They want crypto to have more utility. And to serve that end, they developed an app that allows users to leverage cost dollar averaging - an investment strategy that allows speculators to purchase stocks at a fixed dollar amount regardless of the share price.

WHY DOES BUSHA SUPPORT BITCOIN?

It is Decentralised:

Unlike the banks, no single institution controls the Bitcoin network. It is maintained by a group of volunteer coders and run by an open network of dedicated computers spread around the world.

It is Global:

Bitcoins can be sent across the world.

This also gives investors added flexibility. They can make payments and transfers without needing a credit card or physical cash.

*Before you invest, note that Bitcoin is a risky investment and should be done with the knowledge that one may encounter high financial gains or none.

Nations

BROTHERS & SISTERS

Larissa Munch and other young leaders are sharing their culture and fighting for the rights of their Indigenous communities

At 19 years old, Larissa is proud to be a member of the Nazko First Nation in British Columbia Dakelh (Carrier) and Nehiyaw (Cree).

To share aspects of her culture, she turns to social media.

At present, her content has been liked over one million times. On her channels, she shares her traditional dancing and impressive beadwork.

For those deriding her efforts on social media, her response is unapologetic.

"I decided to bring my traditions to social media because I know people look up to me. I am a huge role model to people. I want to inspire all the youth to engage in their culture. It's important that youth learn about their culture."

Building on this point, Charitie Ropati, a 21 year old from the Native Village of Kongiganak in Alaska. She is working to develop a Native-Centric syllabus. In speaking about her reasons for initiating this project, she draws on her past.

"As an Indigenous student and a member of the Native Village of Kongiganak, Alaska, I never saw myself in the history I learned in primary and secondary school."

Instead of waiting for someone to solve this issue, she began working with noted academics such as Dr. Maria Shaa Williams, Director of the Alaska Studies Department at the University of Alaska Anchorage, and Dr. Richard Manning, professor at the University of Canterbury.

Together they developed an accurate and inclusive history sub curriculum of Indigenous peoples that highlights the traumas faced by her ancestors. Her project leverages readings, videos, movies, and Native guest speakers to investigate events like the Alaska Native Claims Settlement Act and the Boarding School Era.

In discussing the trajectory of her project, she hopes that it will inspire educators, politicians, and legislators to seriously address the concerns of Native communities.

Charitie rejects the notion that young people are powerless. She challenges them to be heard.

"It is no longer OK to accept classes that refuse to acknowledge the histories of Indigenous people. Native students must speak out and educators must listen to our voices. Politicians and legislators must address the issues Native students face. Our voices need to be amplified, especially when it comes to conversations about what we learn."

This sentiment is echoed in the actions of Naelyn Pike, a 21 year old

from the Chiricahua Apache band in Arizona. She leads the Apache Stronghold, which is fighting to stop a mining project that would desecrate sacred land [Oak Flat] - an Apache site.

In a speech that she delivered at a gathering, Naelyn encouraged others to leverage modern tools to fight for their beliefs.

"You think because you're young and you're a woman of colour, that

> "I want education systems to amplify the voices of my ancestors. I want Native youth to feel seen in their classes."

no one's going to hear you. But what was instilled in me, by my ancestors, because they fought for their land and they fought for us to stand here and be here today, [was that] I could also fight. It's not fighting with bows and arrows, and it's not fighting in that kind of sense, but now it's fighting with laws and fighting through paperwork and through speaking out, and going to events and testifying and contacting our congressmen and our leaders of our nation, and so that's what I started to do."

Maintaining a connection with one's ancestors is also important to Jewel

Charles, a 20 year old woman from La Ronge - Northern Saskatchewan. She wrote a book entitled, *Kihci - Kimotan, A Special Secret*. It is a story that follows two young children who go on imaginary adventures involving climbing mountains and being in space. This book is now available in English and Cree.

The reason that Jewel insisted that the book be also translated into Cree was her belief that language is a crucial component of any culture.

Her Grandmother was forced into a residential school, so she never taught Jewel's mother Cree. This also meant that Jewel never learned.

To ensure that more youths have the opportunity that she never had, Jewel suggests that Indigenous languages be included in the curricula across North America.

This way of thinking resonates with Nicholas Flowers. He is a Nunatsiavut high school student that won the STEM Horizon Award. It granted him $25,000 which he will use to pursue a Science degree from Memorial University.
Despite his success, he remains humble and focused on giving back.

"From this point on, I know that I'll do my best to continue to be an ambassador in my community and province to support the field of STEM".

During his last year of high school, he started a program for elementary students to get them excited about STEM subjects.

He also entered and won the first Virtual Science Fair in Newfoundland. His entry used seal oil to power qulliq - a traditional Inuit lamp.

MENTAL
HEALTH

Ose Arheghan is a 22 year old LGBTQ activist. They got involved in mental health advocacy after dealing with their own struggles. Now, their mission is to help others attain peace of mind.

Attending high school was fraught with challenges. But Ose embraced each one. They led the cultural proficiency subcommittee. Many note that this group played a crucial role in changing the school's discrimination policy.

This collective, under Ose's leadership, also published a series of articles on expanding the terms around diversity, sexuality and race. Not satisfied with progress in her state, they traveled to Washington, D.C with the cultural proficiency subcommittee group. Their mission was to lobby Congress for comprehensive sexual education that included LGBTQ teens.

Their experience as a change maker started in grade 8. Ose believes strongly that pushing for change is necessary.

"I had to fight for the rights I didn't have because no one was fighting for them fully for me"

Even though Ose is a huge proponent of living in congruence with yourself, it wasn't an easy path to follow. In describing the process of coming out, Ose doesn't avoid the pain latent in the experience.

"I came out and I use quotation marks for that because my idea of coming out was to start dating people who other people didn't think I should be dating. I had people coming up to me and say 'Well my parents

said I couldn't be friends with you anymore because you're dating this girl and we're not ok with that"

These types of reactions were microaggressions that made Ose feel discriminated against. The accumulation of them began to have an impact on Ose's self-esteem. But instead of being pulled under the tides of despair, Ose fought back.

"There wasn't a way to say I was discriminated against because of my sexuality and I realized there needed to be measures in place so that students would feel protected based on their identities"

As a means of realizing this goal, Ose is planning to attend Ohio State University and double major in political science and sexuality studies.

"I'm hoping to work in politics and not just advocate for LGBTQ rights, but also create legislation that protects LGTQ rights"

Ose advises other young people to seize their own power and create the type of change they desire.

Ose's proactive approach is something that she is quick to try to encourage others to adopt.

"If you have a problem, you're never too small of a person to make a change and speak out"

Ose wants everyone to feel pride - meaning that they are able to live authentically without any remnant of shame. It is a wonderful way to live that everyone deserves.

UPENDO BOOKS LTD

OFFICIAL S...
MI...
FILM FE...
202...
MONTANA INTERNATI...

Rhode
Island
Interna...
Film
Festiva...

202...
BRONZ...
• Film Festival of A...
OFFIC...
SELEC...

Hannah Lucas, a 19 year old from Georgia not only supports Ose's mission, but also understands the importance of helping those struggling to overcome mental health challenges.

At 15, she developed Postural orthostatic tachycardia syndrome (POTS), a condition that causes her to faint.

The fear of succumbing to this condition while being alone caused her to miss 196 classes. She developed debilitating anxiety and depression which led to a suicide attempt. Out of one of her darkest moments, she arrived at an idea to help others.

With the help of her younger brother, Charlie she developed an app called NotOk. It is a free digital panic button that stores up to 5 contacts.

HOW DOES THE NOTOK APP WORK?

Once it is activated, a notice is sent out alerting others to contact the person in distress by text, phone call, or a compassionate visit. The location of the person in distress is also communicated through GPS.

After the crisis is over, the person in distress is able to notify their contacts that the period of turmoil is over.

Hannah remains a compassionate advocate for those suffering from mental health issues. She is acutely aware of the dangers that mental distortions pose and have worked to offset the debilitating effects of shame and isolation.

"Depression and anxiety inhibit a person's ability to ask for help. So, making it EASY for people to ask for help is necessary".

To avoid anxiety or depression, Hannah advises her peers to embrace their flaws. It is important to note that this also means experiencing spectrums of emotion including those that we are sometimes taught to avoid. Rather than fighting to be perfect, Hannah understands that it's perfect to be flawed.

She notes that internalising this belief will help us grow to love our unique selves instead of avoiding our individual experiences.

"It's OK not to be OK. We need to accept our flaws and love ourselves no matter what"

This is a crucial point given that suicide is the 10th leading cause of death among 13-24 year olds.

As a means of combating these grim statistics, Hannah agreed to be featured in a film entitled, Out of the Dark. It was a well received documentary and earned numerous

> "If you want to help someone that is struggling with a mental health issue, think about what you say before saying it"

award nominations.

Miana Bryant, a 21 year old native of Maryland supports Hannah's perspective. She also struggled with depression and anxiety as a teen. To cope with her own challenges as well as help others, Miana created The Mental Elephant in 2016.

It is a non-profit organisation that seeks to empower others through mental health awareness. Miana understands the debilitating effects of isolation, so she made sure that The Mental Elephant facilitated a culture of connection.

"The Mental Elephant is important to me because it provides a space for young adults to speak about their struggles and day-to-day pain"

Miana's larger goal is to expand the current offerings of The Mental Elephant.

"My long-term goal is to provide low-cost therapy sessions and to build physical elephant centers, kind of like how we have YMCA currently where people can go and receive treatment. I want to allow people that are in low-income areas, like small towns, to be able to access proper health care."

If you or someone that you know is struggling with their mental health, feel free to download the NotOK App, direct them to a support group, or help them get into therapy.

Attaining good mental health is possible if we are mindful of the resources that are available to us. The stigma surrounding seeking help to address emotional challenges has significantly dissipated. Those that improve their emotional responses to difficult situations are now regarded as being courageous.

It is crucial to understand that those addressing mental health challenges are not alone. It is believed that almost 800 million people worldwide live with mental health issues.

While this is a daunting reality, we should acknowledge that various forms of treatment are effective. Always remember to handle these types of issues with patience and empathy.

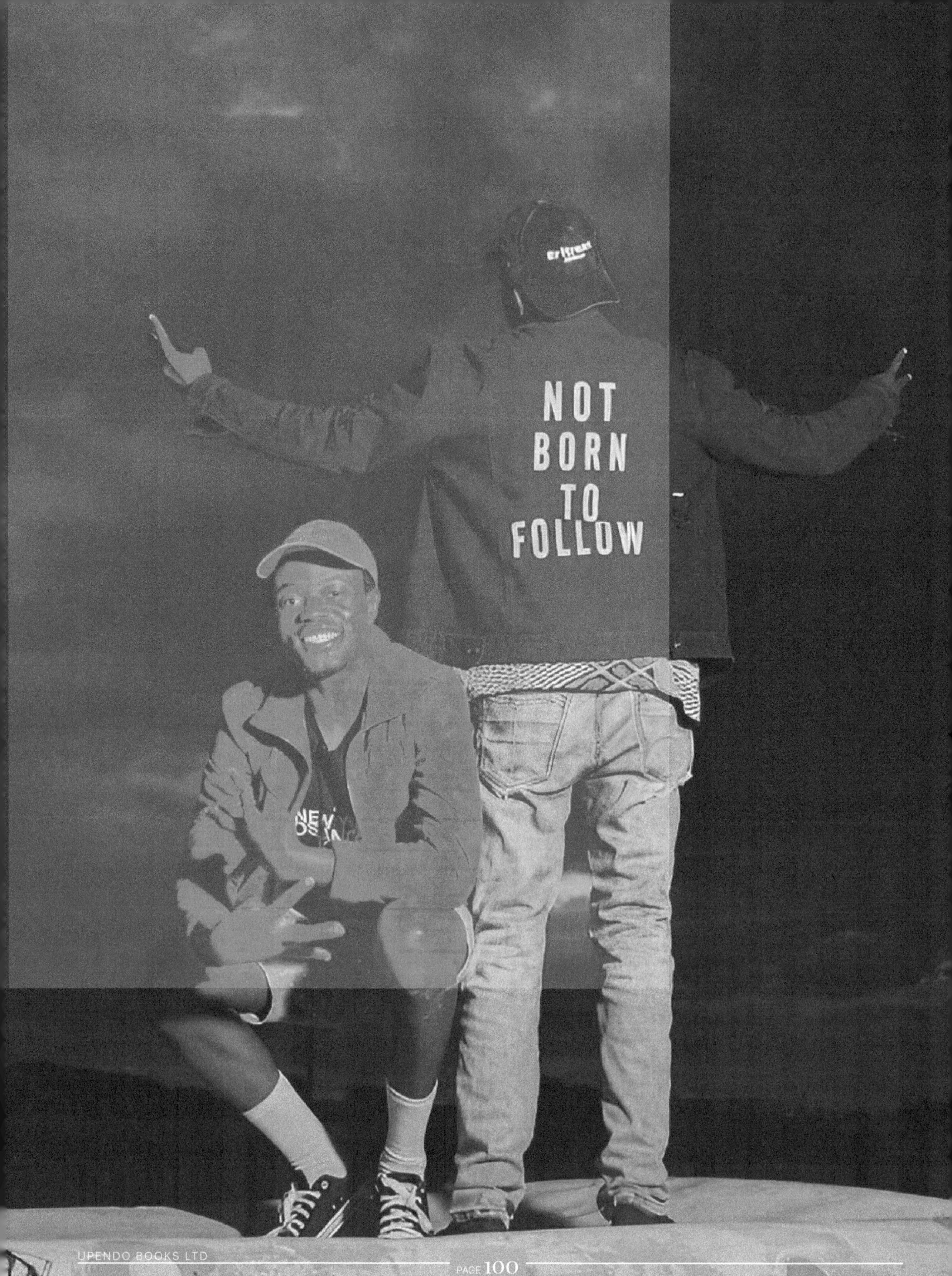
NOT
BORN
TO
FOLLOW

FOCUS ON THE PRESENT MOMENT

I CREATE MY OWN OPPORTUNITIES

I KNOW MY WORTH & SPEAK MY TRUTH

"Some changes look negative on the surface but you Will soon realize that space is being created in your Life for something new to emerge."

-ECKHART TOLLE

OUR
VOICES
RESONATE

HEALING
HACKADAY.COM
PHOTOS- HACKADAY.COM

INVESTING
UPENDO BOOKS LTD -
YOUTUBE INTERVIEW
PHOTOS -
THETRUTHJONES.COM

MOVEMENT
BECAUSEOFTHEM.COM
PHOTOS - AVENUE

BRUSH UP
THEDINNERTABLEDOC.COM
PHOTOS -
THEDINNERTABLEDOC.COM

STEM
ATODAY.ORG
VOYAGEATL.COM
PHOTO - COURTESY OF ALENA
WICKER

IMAGES
THISGENERATION.COM
PHOTO: THISGENERATION.COM

POETRY
GETLIT.ORG
ALORAYOUNG.COM
CLICK2HOUSTON.COM
PHOTOS - FUJI FILM-X.COM,
THE STACKS PODCAST

IDENTITY
SPECTRUMNEWS1.COM
PHOTO - INSTAGRAM

BUSINESSS
ZANDRABEAUTY.COM
PHOTO - BLACKBUSINESS.COM

AFRICAN GENIUS
AFROTECH.COM
PHOTO - MONROEDISPATCH
PHOTO - STIRILEPROTV.RO

DISABILITY
HABENGIRMA.COM
PHOTO - CENTREFORIDEAS.COM

STAY INSPIRED

Anything can be accomplished through hard work, dedication and
CONSISTENCY. Every day concentrate on being just 1% better than you were
the previous day...

THEATRE
MQLIT.CA
ANDSCAPE.COM
PHOTO - FRINGETORONTO
PHOTO - PSWBPORTAITURE.COM

ENVIRONMENT
WAWAGATHARU.ORG
PHOTOS - THEBRIGHTSIDE.COM

TECH
BOREDPANDA.COM
ASSEMBLY.MALALA.ORG
PHOTO - CLOUDMASTERS.ES

ZEN
TABAYATKINS.COM
BDAWSON.CORM
PHOTO -ORANGECOAST.COM ,
GROVECAMPUS.COM

ANIMATION
TEENVOGUE
PHOTOS -TOONBOOMANIMATION

LAW
FREEP.COM
GCPAAWARDS.COM
PHOTOS - FREEP.COM

ARCHITECTURE
HOK.COM
PHOTOS - DAZEENC.OM

FACE VALUE
FREEP.COM

BITCOIN
BUSHA.COM
PHOTO - SUPPLIED

NATIONS
QUEENS OBSERVER.COM
PHOTO - KATE JENSON

MENTAL HEALTH
NBCNEW.COM, PHOTO - YAHOO

Printed in the USA
CPSIA information can be obtained
at www.ICGtesting.com
CBHW061647220724
11983CB00017B/240